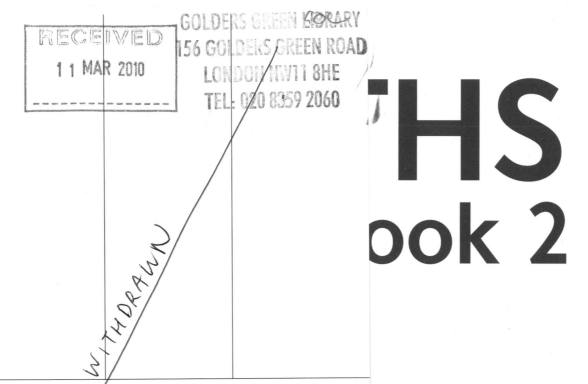

'THS

ook 2

Steve Mills

Watt

Rising Stars UK Ltd, 22 Grafton Street, London W1S 4EX

www.risingstars-uk.com

Every effort has been made to trace copyright holders and obtain their permission for the use of copyright materials. The authors and publisher will gladly receive information enabling them to rectify any error or omission in subsequent editions.

All facts are correct at time of going to press.

Published 2009
Text, design and layout © Rising Stars UK Ltd.

Story author: Tom Watt
Educational authors: Hilary Koll and Steve Mills
Publisher: Jean Carnall
Cover design: Burville-Riley Partnership
Design: Seamonster Design
Illustrations: Seamonster Design/David Woodroffe/Patrick Boyer for Illustration Ltd
Photographs: Getty Images

British Library Cataloguing in Publication Data.
A CIP record for this book is available from the British Library.

ISBN: 978-1-84680-510-3

Printed by Craftprint International Ltd, Singapore

Rising Stars would like to thank Scott Cohen and Alan Sefton of Football in the Community for Arsenal Football Club for their help and support.

Contents

Dear Auntie Ann,

Just wanted to write to say thanks for the birthday present. I used the money to put down a deposit on a car. It's a second-hand Honda. Not a real footballer's car, maybe, but it means I won't have to get the bus into training every morning!

You may have heard from Mum that I've been training with the first team. The Manager says young players will always get a chance while he's the boss at Shelby. Fingers crossed!

This season has been great anyway. I have been playing for the under-19s. That means we have games against some of the big clubs like Liverpool and United. I have also been playing for Town in the FA Youth Cup.

Any time you or Uncle Jack want to come to a game, I'll sort out tickets. Thanks again for the help with the car!

Love,

Stuart

Team Talk

⚽ The football season for most British leagues usually begins in August and runs until May. The home and away matches are usually on alternate weeks.
Can you say the months of the year in order from August to May?

⚽ How many days are in a week? How many months are in a year? How many weeks are in a year?
Do you know how many days are in each month?

Warm Up

▶ **Counting on and back in 7s**

1 Write the missing numbers in each sequence.

a) 7, 14, __, __, 35

b) 3, 10, __, __, 31

c) 5, __, __, __, 33

d) 1, 8, __, __, __,

e) 2, 9, __, __, __,

f) 28, __, __, __, 0

g) 34, __, __, __, 6

h) 32, __, __, __, 4

i) 30, __, __, __, 2

2 Shelby Dynamos won matches on five consecutive Saturdays in October. The first was on 2 October. Write the dates of the other wins.

> **Manager's Message**
> Make sure that the bus arrives before the time Stuart needs to be at Manor Park, not after. It may mean he has to wait around for some time.

Skills Practice 1

▶ **Calculate time intervals and read and interpret timetables**

Stuart Dolan often takes a bus to the Football Academy from his home in Milton Road. Here is the bus timetable.

	Bus 31a	Bus 31b	Bus 31a	Bus 31a	Bus 31b	Bus 31a
Shelby Square	8:20 a.m.	9:15 a.m.	11:20 a.m.	12:50 p.m.	5:15 p.m.	5:50 p.m.
Milton Road	8:25 a.m.	9:20 a.m.	11:25 a.m.	1:55 p.m.	5:20 p.m.	5:55 p.m.
Pannet Park	8:35 a.m.	-	11:35 a.m.	2:05 p.m.	-	6:05 p.m.
Upper Avenue	8:45 a.m.	9:35 a.m.	11:45 a.m.	2:15 p.m.	5:35 p.m.	6:15 p.m.
Lower Avenue	8:50 a.m.	-	11:50 a.m.	2:20 p.m.	-	6:20 p.m.
Manor Park	9:05 a.m.	9:50 a.m.	12:05 p.m.	2:35 p.m.	5:50 p.m.	6:35 p.m.

1 Write the time of the bus from Milton Road that Stuart should take to reach Manor Park by

a) 6:30 p.m.

b) 10:15 a.m.

c) 12:45 p.m.

d) 5:20 p.m.

2 If Stuart takes bus 31a, how long does it take to travel from Milton Road to Manor Park?

3 If Stuart takes bus 31b, how much quicker is it to go from Milton Road to Manor Park than on bus 31a?

Skills Practice 2

▶ Use a calendar to calculate time intervals

The dates of Shelby Town's matches during the first part of the season are shown on this calendar. Each match is marked with a star. Blue means that the match is a home game. Red means it is an away game. Stuart Dolan's birthday is marked with a yellow circle.

September 2008

M	T	W	T	F	S	S
1	2	3	4	5	6	7
8	9	10	11	12	13	14
15	16	17	18	19	20	21
22	23	24	25	26	27	28
29	30					

October 2008

M	T	W	T	F	S	S
		1	2	3	4	5
6	7	8	9	10	11	12
13	14	15	16	17	18	19
20	21	22	23	24	25	26
27	28	29	30	31		

November 2008

M	T	W	T	F	S	S
					1	2
3	4	5	6	7	8	9
10	11	12	13	14	15	16
17	18	19	20	21	22	23
24	25	26	27	28	29	30

December 2008

M	T	W	T	F	S	S
1	2	3	4	5	6	7
8	9	10	11	12	13	14
15	16	17	18	19	20	21
22	23	24	25	26	27	28
29	30	31				

1 Write the day and date/dates of

   a) all the home matches in October

   b) all the away matches in November

   c) Stuart Dolan's birthday

   d) the last match of the year

2 How many days after the 6 September match is

   a) the next match?

   b) the next away match?

   c) the 27 September match?

   d) the 4 October match?

   e) the 25 October match?

   f) the 15 November match?

Game On

Can you work out the dates for each of these matches using the clues below?
Use the calendar to help you.

1 Arsenal v Shelby Town (away)

2 Shelby Town v Liverpool (home)

3 Aston Villa v Shelby Town (away)

4 Shelby Town v West Ham United (home)

5 Shelby Town v Tottenham Hotspur (home)

Clue 1
The away match at Arsenal is exactly 3 weeks after the Saturday match in October at home to Liverpool.

Clue 2
The West Ham United home game is exactly 26 days before the Boxing Day clash away to Aston Villa.

Clue 3
The match at home to Tottenham Hotspur is exactly 71 days before the West Ham United home game.

The Big Match – Season Fixtures

Play this game with a partner.
You will need the Shelby Town cards and a copy of this year's calendar.

Kick-off

- Player A: Choose a date for a match between 1 January and 31 May, e.g. 19 February
- Player B: Pick a Shelby Town card for a number, e.g. 7
- Player A: Decide whether this will be 'weeks' or 'days'
- Player B: Give the date that far on from the chosen date, e.g. seven weeks from 19 February
- If correct, player B scores a point
- Swap roles. Take five goes each
- The winner is the player with most points at the end

Match day programme Shelby Town v Norwich City, September 20, Kick-off 4.00

The Diamond vision

Good afternoon and welcome to Manor Park for another vital Championship game. Tonight's visitors are Norwich City who know all about where we're trying to go: the Premier League. It's been tough for them since they were relegated but City are a great club. I'm sure they'll be back!

One thing I admire about Norwich is a very good record of bringing on their own young players. That's something I want to see us do more of here. I know some people think we should be spending money trying to get promoted. I think our own youngsters can do the job for us. In the FA Youth Cup last week, a lad by the name of Stuart Dolan hit a hat trick against Blackburn. If I had to throw him into a first team game, I wouldn't be worried about him.

Just think about the impact that young lads like Michael Owen, David Beckham and Wayne Rooney have made down the years. They are now international stars. Who's to say that boys at Town like Dolan won't go on to make names for themselves in the game? And save us money, too!

Hope you'll roar the team on to another three points tonight. We're going well right now. And lads like Stuart Dolan are proof that the future looks promising!

Up The Town!

Mick Diamond

Team Talk

⚽ The word 'difference' is used in many ways, such as 'the difference between Beckham and Rooney' or 'the difference in the atmosphere tonight'.
In maths, the word 'difference' has a particular and different meaning.
Do you know what it is?

⚽ How do you find the 'difference' between two numbers?

Warm Up

▶ **Use knowledge of addition and subtraction facts and place value to derive sums and differences of pairs of multiples of 100 or 1000**

Here are the weekly wages of some football players.

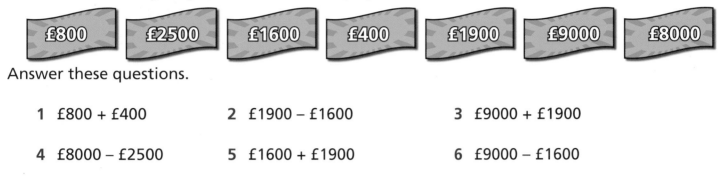

Answer these questions.

1 £800 + £400	2 £1900 – £1600	3 £9000 + £1900
4 £8000 – £2500	5 £1600 + £1900	6 £9000 – £1600

Skills Practice 1

▶ **Use efficient written methods to add whole numbers**

This box shows the number of league appearances made, and goals scored, by Rooney, Beckham and Owen up to 20 September 2008.

Wayne Rooney		Appearances	Goals
2002–2004	Everton	67	15
2004–present	Manchester United	131	53

David Beckham			
1993–2003	Manchester United	265	62
2003–2007	Real Madrid	162	13
2007–present	Los Angeles Galaxy	27	5

Michael Owen			
1996–2004	Liverpool	216	118
2004–2005	Real Madrid	35	13
2005–present	Newcastle United	47	20

1 Find the total number of league goals scored by

    a) Rooney   b) Beckham   c) Owen

2 Find the total number of league appearances made by

    a) Rooney   b) Beckham   c) Owen

Skills Practice 2

▶ Use efficient written methods to subtract whole numbers

This box shows the number of England appearances made, and goals scored, by Beckham, Owen and Rooney up to 20 September 2008.

Wayne Rooney		Appearances	Goals
2004–present	England	46	15

David Beckham			
2004–present	England	105	17

Michael Owen			
2004–present	England	89	40

1 Find how many more England goals Owen has scored than

   a) Rooney   **b)** Beckham

2 Find how many more England appearances Beckham has made than

   a) Rooney   **b)** Owen

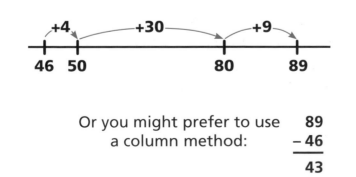

Manager's Message
You might want to find the difference by counting up from the smaller number to the larger number.

$$89 - 46 = 43$$

+4   +30   +9

46   50   80   89

Or you might prefer to use a column method:

$$\begin{array}{r} 89 \\ -\ 46 \\ \hline 43 \end{array}$$

Game On

Use the information on the previous pages to work out the missing numbers in this web page.

Fascinating Football Facts

STFC
ACTA NON VERBA

Home

Manor Park

News

Fixtures

Football Facts

Contact us

- David Beckham and Michael Owen both played for Real Madrid. Beckham made ☐ more league appearances for Real Madrid than Owen.

- Up to 20 September 2008, Rooney has still only made about half the number of appearances at Manchester United as Beckham did. Beckham made ☐ more league appearances for Man United than Rooney so far.

- Up to 20 September 2008, Michael Owen's goal scoring record is impressive. He has scored (for league and for England) a total of ☐ goals, which is ☐ more than Rooney has scored so far.

- Up to September 2008, David Beckham's league and England team appearances are impressive. He has appeared (for league and for England) a total of ☐ times, which is ☐ more than Rooney has appeared so far.

The Big Match – Peter Shilton

Read this football fact:

The record-holder both for the number of league appearances and England appearances is Peter Shilton, who played between 1966 and 1997.
As a goalkeeper, he made 1005 league appearances and 125 England appearances.

Kick-off

- Work with a partner.
- Work out how many more league appearances Beckham, Rooney and Owen would have to make to beat Peter Shilton's league record.
- Now work out how many more England appearances Beckham, Rooney and Owen would have to make to beat Peter Shilton's England record.

Extra Time

⚽ Find the total number of appearances (for league and England) made by Shilton, Beckham, Rooney and Owen.

SPORT

18 August • Daily News

GET YOUR SHIRT ON TOWN!
Bargains at The Manor Ground Superstore!

DOVE 12 BING 22

Special offer on last season's home kit available now:

BUY THE TOWN SHIRT ...
& SOCKS COME FREE!

Get down to Manor Park while stocks last!

Team Talk

⚽ The advert in the match day programme is showing the prices for replica kit.
How much less than £40 is the adult size shirt?

⚽ How much more than £20 is the child size shirt?

Warm Up

▶ Derive and recall multiplication facts up to 10 × 10, the corresponding division facts and multiples of numbers to 10 up to the tenth multiple

1 Eight 5-a-side teams need how many players?

2 One football boot has 9 studs. How many studs are there on 6 boots?

3 Chelsea wins 7 consecutive matches. They score 3 points for each match. How many points is this?

4 Four footballs cost £32. How much does 1 football cost?

5 The match day programme costs £4. How much do 6 programmes cost?

Skills Practice 1

▶ Use place value to multiply whole numbers by 10 and 100

Here are the prices of this season's replica shirts in the Shelby Town shop.

Adult sizes

Shelby Town home kit		Shelby Town away kit		Shelby Town training kit	
SHIRT A	£40	SHIRT B	£39	SHIRT C	£19
SHORTS D	£17	SHORTS E	£20	SHORTS F	£12

Child sizes

Shelby Town home kit		Shelby Town away kit		Shelby Town training kit	
SHIRT A	£25	SHIRT B	£24	SHIRT C	£14
SHORTS D	£11	SHORTS E	£15	SHORTS F	£8

Kit Manager's Message
Remember: When multiplying by 10 or 100, the digits move one or two places to the left.

1 Write the cost of 10 of each item above.

2 Write the cost of 100 of each item above.

Skills Practice 2

▶ Use place value to multiply and divide whole numbers by 10

▶ Solve problems involving money

When the replica shirts are made, letter transfers are used to show the player's name.
It costs 10p extra for each letter of the player's name.

1 How many letters in the player's name if this extra cost is

    a) 40p?   b) 70p?   c) 90p?   d) 110p?   e) £1.20?   f) £1.40?

2 What is the extra cost for these names?

    a) DOLAN   b) EMILIO   c) ODEGBAME   d) MICKLETHWAITE

Game On

▶ Refine and use efficient written methods to add and subtract £.p

A replica shirt costs £2.99 to make.
The small letters for the player's name costs 10p per letter.
The player's number costs 35p per digit.

Work out the price to make each of these shirts.

Extra Time

⚽ Find out how much profit is made on each shirt if the sale price is £39.

The Big Match –
Match Day Programme Adverts

Local companies pay to put adverts in the match day programme. The prices per letter are shown below.

Small font is 10p per letter.

Medium font is 20p per letter.

Large font is 50p per letter.

*   No charge for punctuation

**   Small picture or logo is £2.50

Kick-off

- Find the cost of each of these adverts.

Walter Wall
Carpets

All rugs and carpets half price!

Car Warehouse

New and second-hand cars

Bridge St, Shelby

Saul Black
Electrical lighting

Lower Avenue, Shelby

www.SueHall.co.uk

Been in an accident?
Talk to us. No win, no fee.

- Design an advert for the match day programme that costs exactly £10.

Hiya Dunney,

Sorry you couldn't make the trip. Here's your postcard! Journey over was a bit long and the minibus wasn't the best! But I'm glad I didn't have to organise it all. Or pay for it! We just play, don't we? Our first game in the little tournament is tonight. Wish us luck! Hope your knee's better.

Up The Town!

Stuart

50c

SHELBY TOWN FC

24 BALCOLM DRIVE

SHELBY

LEEDS

Team Talk

⚽ What kinds of things would you need to think about if you were planning a trip to Arnhem?

⚽ How much might it all cost? Will it be necessary to pay for things in pounds or in euros?

Warm Up

▶ Use knowledge of number operations and corresponding inverses, including doubling and halving, to estimate and check calculations

1 You'll be using the office computer to help you organise the Arnhem trip. Unfortunately, it has a bug and keeps making mistakes. Check which are wrong by doubling the answers. Write the correct answer if it is wrong.

   a) Half of 44 is 22   b) Half of 52 is 26   c) Half of 54 is 22

   d) Half of 72 is 31   e) Half of 98 is 49   f) Half of 58 is 24

2 Halve the answers to check these.

   a) Double 18 is 46   b) Double 45 is 80   c) Double 36 is 612

   d) Double 49 is 99   e) Double 46 is 92   f) Double 38 is 56

Skills Practice 1

▶ Use efficient written methods of calculation, including addition and subtraction of decimals

Travel Manager's Message
Remember to add the taxes and take off the discount.

Per person
London Stansted to Niederrhein Airport
Outgoing flight on 27/09 ....£37.50
Incoming flight on 29/09 ....£43.32
Plus taxes and booking fee of.....................£54.20

£7.25 discount per person if booking online

1 Find the total cost per person of booking return flights online.

2 Find the cost for 20 return flights booked online.

3 Find the cost for 5 return flights booked online.

4 Find the cost for 25 return flights booked online.

Skills Practice 2

▶ Use written methods to calculate TU x U and HTU x U

Look at these coach and minibus adverts. You will need transport for twenty-five people for two days (48 hours). Work out which is the cheapest option and how much it would cost. The prices are shown in pounds.

Van Persie Vans
50-seater coach
£285 per day

Der Meer Minibuses
13-seater Minibus
£6 per hour

Minibus Hire
10-seater Minibus
£187 for 2 days

Herts Van Rental
40-seater coach
£279 per day

Game On

You will also need to have hotel accommodation. These prices are shown in euros.

1 Copy this table, giving each price in pounds.

Hotel Arnie	
Double/Twin room	€90
Single room	€60
Breakfast	€15
Evening meal	€25

Manager's Message
To convert approximately from euros into pounds – multiply by 8 and then divide by 10.

2 Find out the cost in pounds of a single room plus breakfast and evening meal for one person.

3 Find out the cost in pounds for two people sharing a twin room including breakfast and evening meals.

The Big Match – Final Booking

Work with a partner. You can use a calculator.

Kick-off

- Using the information on the previous pages, work out the total cost for the following.

> **Travel Manager's Message**
> Make sure all your amounts are worked out in pounds.

- Return flights, booked online, for 25 people

- One coach rented from Herts Van Rental for 2 days

- 1 single room for 2 nights at Hotel Arnie

- 12 twin rooms for 2 nights at Hotel Arnie

- Breakfasts and evening meals for 25 people for 2 days

- Give your answer in pounds.
- To this total, add £35 per person to cover lunches, snacks and other expenses.
- Each person should pay an equal share. There are twenty-five people. How much should each pay? Round your answer to the nearest pound.

Match day programme Shelby Town v Cardiff, 30 August, Kick-off 4.00

13 August
Captain's Message

Welcome to Manor Park. Thanks for your fantastic support at the last home game: 2-0 down to Norwich and coming back to win 3-2. We'd never have done it without you! Hope it won't be quite so nail-biting tonight, although Cardiff are another good side.

I've been enjoying training lately. As you may know, I'm doing my coaching badges at the moment. The boss has let me put on sessions for the younger lads like Stuart Dolan, Sam Cohen and Mark Bing. The boys are great to work with. We have been working on our passing and getting a good pattern in our play. Football is all about knowing what's supposed to happen next, I think.

Enjoy the game tonight. If any of those young lads get a game tonight, remember, it's Dave Morgan who's taught them everything they know!

Up The Town!

Dave Morgan

Team Talk

⚽ If players with numbered shirts pass the ball from one to another, patterns can be formed with the shirt numbers.

⚽ What patterns could these be? Who would be passed to next?

⚽ What about these patterns? 1, 3, 5, 7, … or 2, 5, 8, 11, … or 1, 4, 9, 16, …

Warm Up

▶ Recognise and continue number sequences formed by counting on or back in steps of constant size

At the training ground, players are passing the ball to each other according to their shirt numbers, using a particular rule. Continue the sequences by writing the next four numbers.

1 1, 4, 7, 10, ...

2 2, 6, 10, 14, ...

3 24, 23, 22, 21, ...

4 24, 22, 20, 18, ...

5 1, 6, 11, 16, ...

6 2, 5, 8, 11, ...

7 24, 21, 18, 15, ...

8 24, 20, 16, ...

9 3, 7, 11, 15, ...

10 23, 21, 19, 17, ...

11 22, 19, 16, ...

12 26, 22, 18, ...

Skills Practice 1

▶ Recognise and describe number patterns and relationships including multiple and square

1 Cones numbered 1 to 6 are placed in a line. Players stand next to the cones, depending on the rule given. Can you work out the rule given for each line of players?

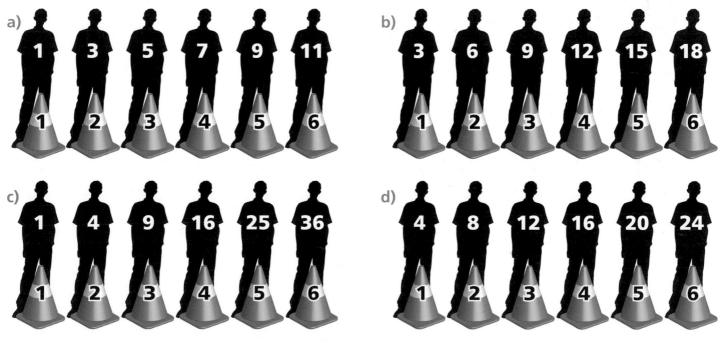

2 If a seventh and eighth cone were placed in the line, which shirt numbers would be needed for each line?

Skills Practice 2

▶ Recognise relationships including multiple, factor and square

As part of training, players are asked questions about their shirt numbers. If they answer 'yes', they must run across the pitch and back. These are the questions.

a multiple of 3?

a square number?

a factor of 24?

a multiple of 7?

a factor of 54?

Work out which of these players will run the furthest.

Manager's Message
A factor is a number that divides exactly into another without leaving a remainder.

DOLAN 8

RILEY 14

LAMBROU 24

ODEGBAME 9

HANNESEN 6

MICKLETHWAITE 21

Game On

For another training exercise, all the players numbered 1 to 24 must get into two groups. If these rules were used to get them into two groups, which players would be in each group? Use the Shelby Town cards to help you sort them into groups.

Group 1A	Group 1B
Factors of 24	Not factors of 24

Group 2A	Group 2B
Multiples of 4	Not multiples of 4

Group 3A	Group 3B
Square numbers	Not square numbers

Group 4A	Group 4B
Factors of 36	Not factors of 36

Can you think of rules for two groups that would have an equal number of players in each group?

The Big Match

Work with a partner or in a small group.
You will need the Shelby Town cards for this game and some counters or cubes.

Kick-off

- Each player should pick a card showing a Shelby Town player's shirt number.
- Each player must answer all the questions in the list below for the card they picked.
- Each time the answer is 'yes' the player picks a counter or cube.
- As a record, each player should write their number down and show how many counters or cubes they won.
- Take five turns each.
- The winner is the player with the most counters or cubes at the end.

Is it a multiple of 4?

Is it a square number?

Is it a factor of 32?

Is it a factor of 48?

Is it a multiple of 7?

Is it an even number?

Is it a multiple of 5?

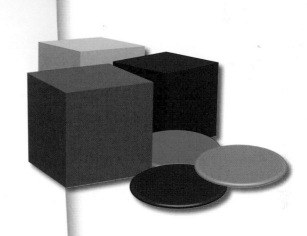

Extra Time

⚽ Which Shelby Town card/cards scores
- the most points?
- the fewest points?

Welcome back to Ford Wednesday Night Football on TalkSport. Back to the Champions League reaction in a moment but first let's go to Manor Park. That re-arranged Carling Cup tie between Shelby Town and Bolton Wanderers went to extra time and penalties. The hero was the Town sub keeper Peter Jenks who saved from Kevin Davies and Kevin Nolan to put Shelby through. Well done, Peter! Let's cross there now and talk to the man himself.

Thanks, Danny. Great night for us.

Absolutely. To save two out of five penalties is great for a keeper. Have you been practising them all week?

Yeah. We knew it would be close tonight. There's a young lad here at Town named Stuart Dolan. Every day after training he fires pens in at me.

He's good at penalties this lad, is he?

Very good. 9 out of 10 on target. If I can save a quarter of Stuart's penalties, I reckon I can save at least half of anybody else's!

Well, two out of five did the trick tonight! Great win for Shelby. Good luck in round four, Peter. Well done and thanks for joining us on TalkSport.

Team Talk

⚽ The keeper, Peter Jenks, saves 'two out of five penalties'. How would you write this as a fraction? If he faces 20 penalties, how many will he save?

⚽ Stuart Dolan gets '9 out of 10 penalty strikes on target'. How would you write this as a fraction? If he strikes 30 penalties, how many will be on target?

Warm Up

▶ Use fractions to describe proportions of a whole

A football match is 90 minutes long. Jim MacDonald, the goalkeeper, is brought on as a substitute to take part in the game.

1 Using the denominator 90, write what fraction of the whole match he played if he was on the pitch for

a) 15 minutes

b) 10 minutes

c) 30 minutes

d) 45 minutes

e) 25 minutes

f) 9 minutes

2 Talk with a partner about whether any other fractions could be used to describe each of those you have written.

Skills Practice 1

▶ Recognise when two fractions are equivalent

Which of these statements do you think are true, and which are false?

1 $\frac{45}{90}$ is equivalent to $\frac{1}{2}$

2 $\frac{30}{90}$ is equivalent to $\frac{1}{3}$

3 $\frac{10}{90}$ is equivalent to $\frac{1}{9}$

4 $\frac{9}{90}$ is equivalent to $\frac{1}{8}$

5 $\frac{70}{90}$ is equivalent to $\frac{7}{9}$

6 $\frac{81}{90}$ is equivalent to $\frac{9}{10}$

7 $\frac{25}{90}$ is equivalent to $\frac{5}{18}$

8 $\frac{15}{90}$ is equivalent to $\frac{1}{6}$

Manager's Message
To check whether two fractions are equivalent, see if you can multiply or divide the top and bottom number by the same number to make the other fraction, like this

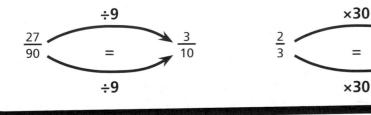

Skills Practice 2

▶ **Solve problems involving proportions**

Here are some goalkeeper statistics.

Goalkeeper	Penalty kicks faced	Penalty kicks blocked	Shots faced	Shots saved
MacDonald	12	3	100	80
Ramos	48	6	96	60
Jenks	15	3	150	105
Mickel	24	8	125	75
Hampton	18	3	48	36

For each of these questions, give each fraction in its simplest form.

1 What proportion of penalties faced were blocked by

    a) MacDonald?   b) Ramos?   c) Jenks?   d) Mickel?   e) Hampton?

2 What proportion of shots faced were saved by

    a) MacDonald?   b) Ramos?   c) Jenks?   d) Mickel?   e) Hampton?

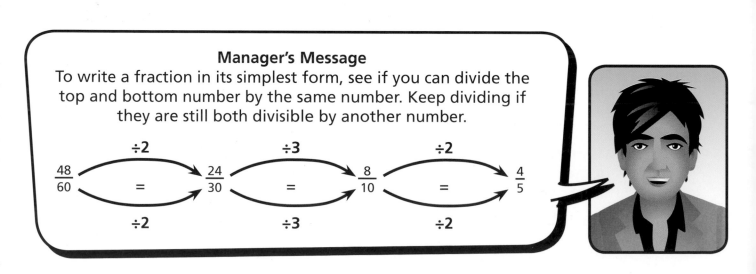

Manager's Message
To write a fraction in its simplest form, see if you can divide the top and bottom number by the same number. Keep dividing if they are still both divisible by another number.

$$\frac{48}{60} \xrightarrow{\div 2} = \frac{24}{30} \xrightarrow{\div 3} = \frac{8}{10} \xrightarrow{\div 2} = \frac{4}{5}$$

Game On

1 Use the fraction comparison chart to help you write the fractions from Question 1 in order of size, starting with the largest.

2 Use the fraction comparison chart to help you write the fractions from Question 2 in order of size, starting with the largest.

Talk to a partner about which of the goalkeepers you think has the best record.

The Big Match – Pitch Fractions

Play this game with a partner.

You will need a dice and the Shelby Town cards marked with these numbers:

6, 8, 10, 12, 16, 20.

Kick-off

● Each pick a card. This tells you the denominator (bottom number) of your fraction.

● Each roll the dice. This tells you the numerator (top number) of your fraction.

● Use the diagram below to compare your two fractions. The player with the larger fraction scores a goal. If the two fractions are equivalent, you both score a goal.

● Record each go using the greater than, less than, or equals signs (<, >, =).

● The winner is the first player to score six goals.

one whole																			
$\frac{1}{2}$										$\frac{1}{2}$									
$\frac{1}{3}$						$\frac{1}{3}$						$\frac{1}{3}$							
$\frac{1}{4}$					$\frac{1}{4}$					$\frac{1}{4}$					$\frac{1}{4}$				
$\frac{1}{5}$				$\frac{1}{5}$				$\frac{1}{5}$				$\frac{1}{5}$				$\frac{1}{5}$			
$\frac{1}{6}$			$\frac{1}{6}$			$\frac{1}{6}$			$\frac{1}{6}$			$\frac{1}{6}$			$\frac{1}{6}$				
$\frac{1}{8}$		$\frac{1}{8}$		$\frac{1}{8}$		$\frac{1}{8}$		$\frac{1}{8}$		$\frac{1}{8}$		$\frac{1}{8}$		$\frac{1}{8}$					
$\frac{1}{10}$	$\frac{1}{10}$	$\frac{1}{10}$	$\frac{1}{10}$	$\frac{1}{10}$	$\frac{1}{10}$	$\frac{1}{10}$	$\frac{1}{10}$	$\frac{1}{10}$	$\frac{1}{10}$										
$\frac{1}{12}$	$\frac{1}{12}$	$\frac{1}{12}$	$\frac{1}{12}$	$\frac{1}{12}$	$\frac{1}{12}$	$\frac{1}{12}$	$\frac{1}{12}$	$\frac{1}{12}$	$\frac{1}{12}$	$\frac{1}{12}$	$\frac{1}{12}$								
$\frac{1}{16}$	$\frac{1}{16}$	$\frac{1}{16}$	$\frac{1}{16}$	$\frac{1}{16}$	$\frac{1}{16}$	$\frac{1}{16}$	$\frac{1}{16}$	$\frac{1}{16}$	$\frac{1}{16}$	$\frac{1}{16}$	$\frac{1}{16}$	$\frac{1}{16}$	$\frac{1}{16}$	$\frac{1}{16}$	$\frac{1}{16}$				
$\frac{1}{20}$	$\frac{1}{20}$	$\frac{1}{20}$	$\frac{1}{20}$	$\frac{1}{20}$	$\frac{1}{20}$	$\frac{1}{20}$	$\frac{1}{20}$	$\frac{1}{20}$	$\frac{1}{20}$	$\frac{1}{20}$	$\frac{1}{20}$	$\frac{1}{20}$	$\frac{1}{20}$	$\frac{1}{20}$	$\frac{1}{20}$	$\frac{1}{20}$	$\frac{1}{20}$	$\frac{1}{20}$	$\frac{1}{20}$

Name: .... Stuart Dolan
DOB: .... 23 March 1990
Nationality: .... UK
Born: .... Shelby
Height: .... 1.8 metres
Weight: ..... 70.3 kilograms

Stuart Dolan starred for Town in last season's FA Youth Cup, scoring five goals in the run to the quarter-finals. Stuart is a local boy who has come up through the ranks at Manor Park. Quick, clever and a natural goalscorer. He may be knocking on the door for a first team call-up this season.

Team Talk

⚽ Which different units of measurement can we use to measure a person's height? What units could be used for a person's weight?

⚽ Can you name different pieces of equipment that we can use to measure a person's height and weight?

Warm Up

▶ **Read scales including reading between labelled divisions**

Write the weight of each boot in grams.

Skills Practice 1

▶ **Use, partition and order decimal numbers**

▶ **Add and subtract decimals**

Some weights of other football boots are given (per boot) in kilograms.

| 0.2 kg | 0.15 kg | 0.23 kg |
| 0.21 kg | 0.3 kg | 0.19 kg |

1 Copy each decimal, underlining the tenths digit.

2 Write the decimals in order of heaviness, starting with the lightest.

3 In wet weather, each boot weighs 0.05 kg more. Write the new weights for each boot.

4 Find the total weight of the six boots listed above.

5 How much lighter is the lightest boot than the heaviest?

Skills Practice 2

▶ **Read scales including reading between labelled divisions**
▶ **Use decimal notation to record measurements (e.g. 1.3 m or 0.6 kg)**

Stuart Dolan is being monitored by the fitness team. He is being weighed and measured in different ways.

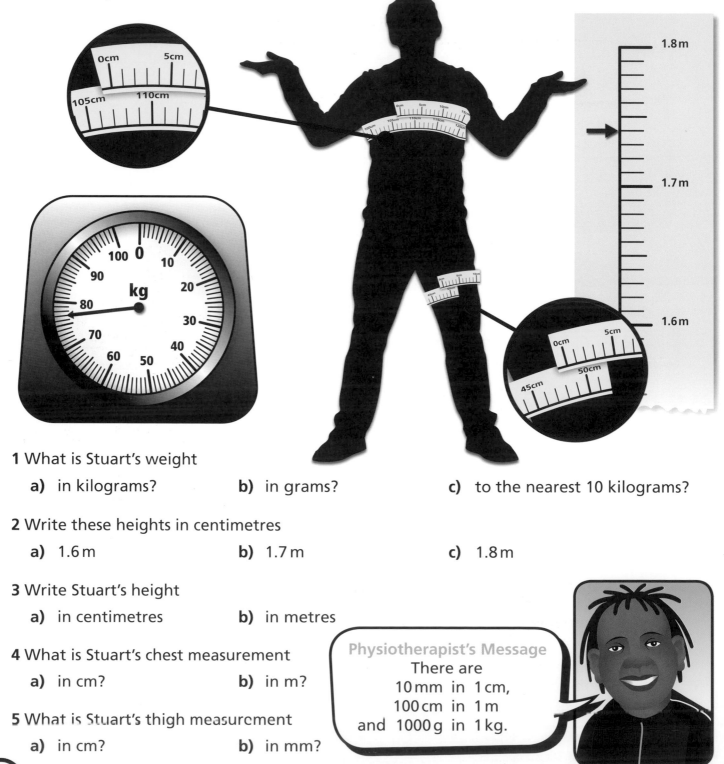

1 What is Stuart's weight

  a) in kilograms?   **b)** in grams?   **c)** to the nearest 10 kilograms?

2 Write these heights in centimetres

  a) 1.6 m   **b)** 1.7 m   **c)** 1.8 m

3 Write Stuart's height

  a) in centimetres   **b)** in metres

4 What is Stuart's chest measurement

  a) in cm?   **b)** in m?

5 What is Stuart's thigh measurement

  a) in cm?   **b)** in mm?

Physiotherapist's Message
There are
10 mm in 1 cm,
100 cm in 1 m
and 1000 g in 1 kg.

Game On

You will need a set of weighing scales and a range of different shoes and boots, labelled A to F.

1 Find out how heavy each shoe and boot is. Give your measurements both in grams and in kilograms.

2 Write the weights in order, starting with the heaviest.

3 Write five true statements about your measurement, like this

Shoe A is 0.1 kg heavier than shoe F.

Shoe B is 150 g lighter than shoe D.

The Big Match – Your Own Measurements

You will need a tape measure for this activity.

Kick-off

- Use a tape measure to measure your own body.
- Record your measurements for all the parts of the body shown in the diagram.
- Give your measurements both in centimetres and in metres.
- Write some statements about how the different parts of your body compare, like this

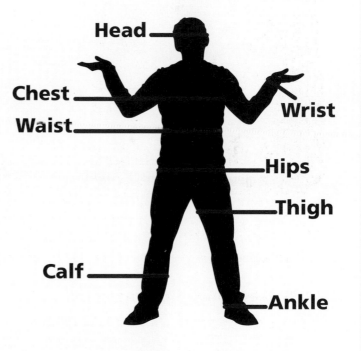

Head

Chest

Waist

Wrist

Hips

Thigh

Calf

Ankle

My chest measurement is 0.3 m larger than my thigh measurement.

The length around my ankle is 15 cm shorter than the length around my calf.

NOW SPORTS

Liverpool	Team statistics	Shelby Town
52%	Possession %	48%
44%	Ball in Shelby half/ Ball in Liverpool half %	56%
3	Goals	1
1	First half goals	1
7	Shots on target	3
12	Shots off target	8
6	Blocked shots	9
5	Corners	5
4	Fouls	16
3	Offsides	9
1	Yellow cards	4
0	Red cards	0

Well, Richard. Those figures tell their own story. Shelby Town have played really well today but it's goals that win games. The Premier League new boys just don't have the cutting edge compared to a team like Liverpool. Plenty of positives for Mick Diamond but Rafa's boys deserved all three points. They look in devastating form at the minute!

Team Talk

⚽ What does it mean when people say 'We'll be giving 100%' or 'there's a 50% chance that he'll be fit for the match'?

⚽ What does % mean? In what other ways can you describe these percentages?

Warm Up

▶ **Understand simple percentages**
▶ **Recall integer complements to 100**

These clothing labels are from the different items in the Shelby Town replica kit.
The total of all the percentages on each label is 100%.

Write the missing percentage from each label.

1	2	3	4	5
50% cotton __ nylon	20% cotton __ silk	40% wool __ nylon 30% silk	45% polyester 15% cotton __ nylon	75% wool __ nylon 10% cotton

Skills Practice 1

▶ **Use percentages to describe proportions of a whole**

During the match, Now Sports shows information about which team has had more possession of the ball in the last five minutes. They also show information about what proportion of the time the ball has spent in each half of the pitch.

Liverpool	Team statistics	Shelby Town
52%	Possession %	48%
44%	Ball in Shelby half/Ball in Liverpool half %	56%

Write the percentages missing from each table for other periods in the match.

1

Liverpool	Team statistics	Shelby Town
15%	Possession %	?%
?%	Ball in Shelby half/Ball in Liverpool half %	34%

2

Liverpool	Team statistics	Shelby Town
68%	Possession %	?%
?%	Ball in Shelby half/Ball in Liverpool half %	27%

3

Liverpool	Team statistics	Shelby Town
41%	Possession %	?%
?%	Ball in Shelby half/Ball in Liverpool half %	82%

Skills Practice 2

▶ Find equivalent percentages and fractions

Use these number lines to help you find equivalent fractions and percentages.

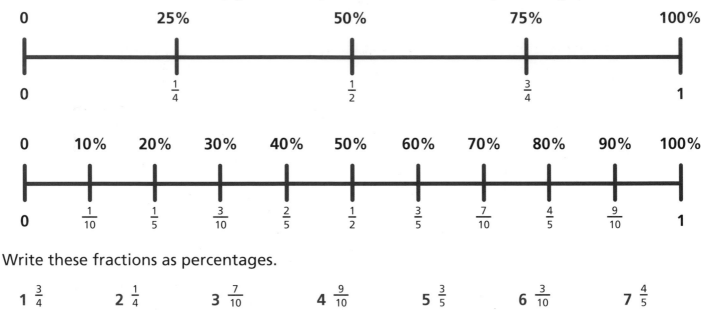

Write these fractions as percentages.

1 $\frac{3}{4}$ **2** $\frac{1}{4}$ **3** $\frac{7}{10}$ **4** $\frac{9}{10}$ **5** $\frac{3}{5}$ **6** $\frac{3}{10}$ **7** $\frac{4}{5}$

Game On

1 Write each statement using percentages.

a Shelby scored 1 out of the 2 goals in the first half.   *Shelby scored 50% of the goals in the first half.*

b Shelby scored 1 out of the 4 goals in the match.

c Shelby made 3 of the 10 shots on target.

d Shelby were given 4 out of the 5 yellow cards.

e Shelby won 5 out of 10 of the corners.

f Shelby had 9 out of the 15 blocked shots.

g Shelby made 8 of the 20 shots off target.

h Shelby had 9 out of the 12 offsides.

i Shelby made 16 of the 20 fouls.

2 Now write the same statements about Liverpool, using percentages.

> **Manager's Message**
> Write the fraction in its simplest form first and then find it on one of the number lines.

The Big Match – Shelby Town's Corners

Play this game with a partner.
You will need some counters.

These boxes show the percentage of corners Shelby Town won in different matches.

50% of 20 corners	25% of 4 corners	75% of 8 corners	10% of 30 corners	20% of 20 corners
10% of 20 corners	50% of 10 corners	30% of 20 corners	25% of 8 corners	20% of 15 corners
50% of 12 corners	60% of 10 corners	25% of 12 corners	10% of 10 corners	30% of 10 corners
90% of 10 corners	75% of 4 corners	80% of 10 corners	70% of 20 corners	25% of 16 corners

Kick-off

- Each player chooses a square. Work out how many corners Shelby Town won.

- The player with the higher answer wins a point. Place a counter to cover the squares you used.

- If they are the same, choose two new squares, without covering the other ones.

- The winner is the first player to win ten points.

Manager's Message
Think of the percentage as a fraction.
75% of 20 is $\frac{3}{4}$ of 20.
Find the fraction.
$\frac{1}{4}$ of 20 is 5, so $\frac{3}{4}$ of 20 is 15.

Most Visited ▾   Getting Started   Latest Headlines

https://www.shelby.premiumtv.co.uk

FOOTIE TALK

Home

News

Message Board

Contact us

Today's thread: What about the draw for the Cup quarter-finals? Who'll go through?

Comment by ST*TILL*DIE
(Posted 38 minutes ago)

Leeds away for us? We have a good chance. If it was at home, I'd say certain but, at Elland Road? 50:50 chance at least! Come on The Town!

Comment by Geordie ST
(Posted 35 minutes ago)

When are tickets on sale? Very likely I'll go. Elland Road's near me but am I likely to get a ticket? Absolute definite that we'll win! Leeds have no chance. Town are Premier League now!

Comment by northstandgus
(Posted 32 minutes ago)

Geordie: unlikely they'll sell out. You'll have a fair chance of getting in on the night. And it's very likely you'll see us make the semis! Up The Town!

Done

Team Talk

⚽ How many words can you find in the description that describe how likely things are to happen?

Warm Up

▶ **Understand the language of probability and likelihood**

Say whether the statements in each pair are describing the same probabilities.

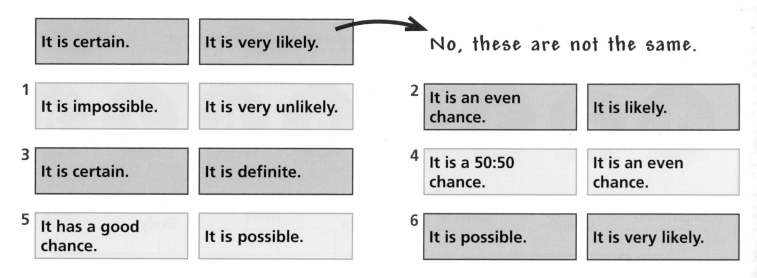

| It is certain. | It is very likely. | No, these are not the same. |

1 It is impossible. | It is very unlikely.

2 It is an even chance. | It is likely.

3 It is certain. | It is definite.

4 It is a 50:50 chance. | It is an even chance.

5 It has a good chance. | It is possible.

6 It is possible. | It is very likely.

Skills Practice 1

▶ **Describe the occurrence of familiar events using the language of chance or likelihood**

We use the words below when describing the probability of something or how likely it is to happen.

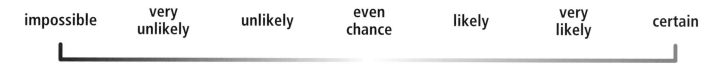

impossible   very unlikely   unlikely   even chance   likely   very likely   certain

Talk to a partner. Decide on a word to describe the probability of each of these events.

1 It is _____ that Shelby Town will win at least one match this year.

2 Stuart's leg injury means that it is _____ that he will play on Saturday.

3 It is _____ that Shelby Town will win all of their matches.

4 There is an _____ that Mick Diamond's new baby will be a boy.

5 It is _____ that the day after Shelby Town's next match, which is on Saturday, is Sunday.

6 It is _____ that all the teams in the league will win all of their matches this season.

Calling all Junior Town members!

SIMPLY THE BEST
(COMPETITION EVER, THAT IS!)

Now's your chance to get out on the pitch with the stars of our first team. Join Stuart Dolan, Dotun Odegbame and Pierre Jean Vert and the boys in training at Manor Park!

It's a fantastic competition. It's exclusive to Junior Town supporters and there are just ten places up for grabs. Winners will be part of 'training triangles' for the morning with top Town stars. Practice your skills: keep-ball, one-twos, angling your runs and crosses, shooting from narrow angles, passing the ball wide to the wingers. You'll learn the pros' secrets! And then join the boys in the canteen for lunch and a chat with the boss, Mick Diamond.

To be a winner, all you have to do is write a 100-word match report about last weekend's game against Aston Villa. Send it in, or e-mail it, to us here at the Club and you could be on your way to the training ground to join the first team for the day. But hurry! Entries must be received by Friday 26th.

Good luck!

Team Talk

⚽ What is an angle? How do we measure it?

⚽ Can you make up a football sentence using the word 'angle'?

Warm Up

▶ Recall facts in the x6, x7, x8, x9 tables

1 6 x 8	2 7 x 4	3 3 x 8	4 9 x 6
5 7 x 6	6 8 x 9	7 7 x 8	8 8 x 8

Skills Practice 1

▶ Compare and order angles less than 180°

On the training ground, passing and shooting drills are set up.

1 In the drills below, say whether each angle is **acute** or **obtuse**.

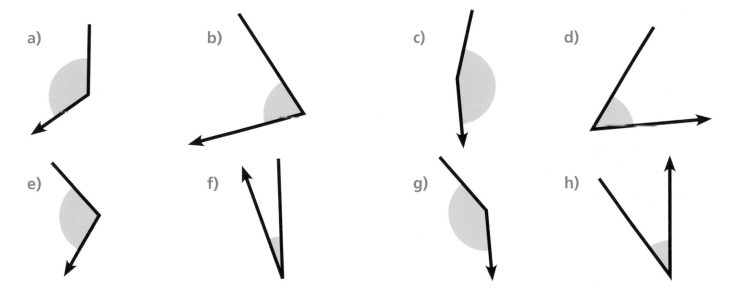

2 Now write the letters to show the angles in order of size, starting with the largest.

Youth Team Coach's Message
An angle is an amount of turn. Acute angles are angles smaller than right angles (between 0 and 90 degrees). Obtuse angles are angles between a right angle and a straight angle (between 90 and 180 degrees).

Skills Practice 2

▶ Know that angles are measured in degrees and that one whole turn is 360°
▶ Begin to estimate angles

Stuart Dolan is standing on the spot and doing some twisting and turning exercises. Estimate the angle he has turned in degrees.

Youth Team Coach's Message
Remember that there are 360° in one full turn, 180° in one half turn and 90° in a quarter turn.

Game On

The players stand in a circle for one drill with the coach in the middle.

The coach receives the ball from a player and then turns clockwise to pass it to another.

Write down how many degrees the coach turns through each time, if he turns from

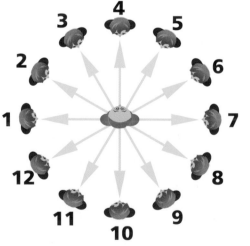

1 2 to 5	2 5 to 7	3 7 to 8
4 8 to 2	5 2 to 6	6 6 to 11
7 11 to 12	8 12 to 3	9 3 to 9

Youth Team Coach's Message
The angle between adjacent players in the diagram is 30°.

The Big Match – A Good Turn

Play this game with a partner.
You need the Shelby Town cards marked from 1 to 12.

Kick-off

- Spread the cards face down on the table. Both players should pick two cards.
- Using the diagram above, work out how many degrees the coach should turn through to go from one number to the other. The coach can turn clockwise or anticlockwise but the angle must be 180° or less.
- The player with the smaller angle scores a point.
- Replace the cards and mix them up on the table.
- Repeat five times.
- The winner is the player with the most points at the end.

Extra Time

⚽ You can play the game again, but this time the coach must turn clockwise, so some of the angles will be greater than 180°.

Still waiting for our first goal. Shelby Town 0 Middlesbrough 0 with fifteen minutes to go. And I'm freezing, folks! Absolutely freezing!

Yes, Alan. We're up on this gantry and the wind's blowing a gale. Makes it difficult to control the ball down on the pitch, too. Young Stuart Dolan was unlucky there when the ball bobbled away from him.

Does it have a real effect on the players when it's this cold, Scott?

Well, look, Alan. Dotun Odegbame's just gone down. That tackle will have hurt even more because it's freezing out there.

And he's from Nigeria, Scott, remember. It's not cold like this over there, is it?

True, Alan. Although he had that spell on loan at Torpedo Moscow while he was with Benfica. And Russia gets a lot colder than this. I know: I played there for Chelsea once.

Well, young Dolan's helping his strike partner to his feet. Between them, they need to come up with a goal. That might warm the crowd up!

Team Talk

⚽ What unit is temperature measured in? Do you know how cold the temperature is when water freezes?

⚽ What do you think the temperature is today? What temperature would it be if it was 25° colder?

Warm Up

▶ **Continue sequences involving negative numbers**

Write the next four numbers in each sequence

1 -5, -4, -3, -2, —, —, —, —,

2 7, 6, 5, 4, 3, 2, 1, —, —, —, —,

3 -3, -4, -5, -6, -7, —, —, —, —,

4 -9, -8, -7, -6, —, —, —, —,

5 4, 3, 2, 1, 0, —, —, —, —,

6 -24, -23, -22, -21, —, —, —, —

Skills Practice 1

▶ **Order and position negative numbers**

It is a very cold winter's day at Manor Park. The thermometer is showing a temperature below freezing.

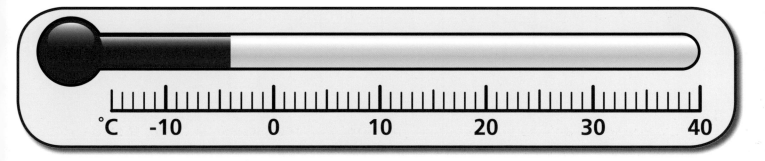

1 What temperature does this thermometer show?

2 The temperature rises by 3°C. What is the new temperature?

3 Yesterday the temperature fell from 7°C to –2°C. How many degrees did it fall?

4 Last week the temperature was 6°C. It fell by 9°C. What was the temperature then?

5 Look at the thermometer. How much must the temperature rise to reach 5°C?

6 What is the difference in temperature between –3°C and 13°C?

Skills Practice 2

▶ **Find differences between positive and negative numbers**

Here are some pairs of temperatures recorded at Shelby Town at different times of the year.
Count on or back along the number line to find the difference between

1   4°C and –1°C   2   9°C and –3°C   3   –9°C and –2°C
4   –2°C and –7°C   5   2°C and –6°C   6   5°C and –8°C

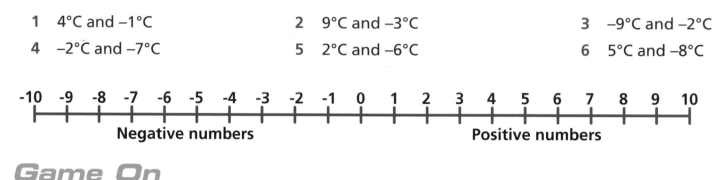

Game On

▶ **Interpret line graphs**

This line graph shows the average monthly temperature (in °C) in Shelby and in Moscow.

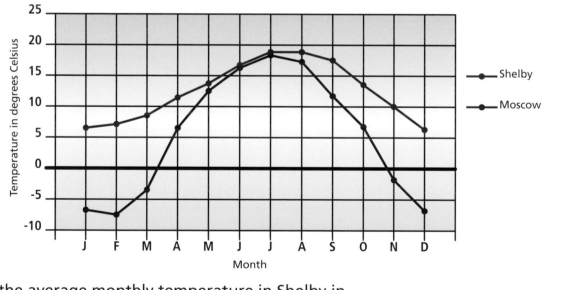

1 What is the average monthly temperature in Shelby in

   a) January?   b) June?   c) September?   d) November?

2 What is the average monthly temperature in Moscow in

   a) January?   b) February?   c) March?   d) November?

3 What is the difference in average monthly temperature between Moscow and Shelby in

   a) January?   b) March?   c) May?   d) October?

4 How many degrees below freezing is the Moscow temperature in December?

The Big Match – Pitch Coordinates

Play this game with a friend. You will need a counter and a dice.
Draw a large number line with numbers from -10 to 10.
10 and -10 are the goals of a football pitch. The centre spot is at zero.

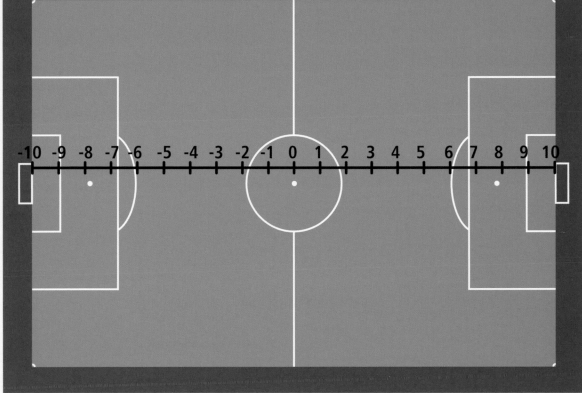

Kick-off

- Place the counter at zero.

- Take turns to roll the dice and move the counter towards your goal.
  One player moves to the left towards -10 and the other moves to the
  right towards 10.

- As each turn is taken, record the movement like this:

At -5. Moved on 3 to -2.
At -2. Moved back 5 to -7.

- When a player reaches 10 or -10 they score a goal.
- The winner is the player with the most goals at the end.

NOW SPORTS

Bendtner

Vela

Nasri

Diaby

Fabregas

Walcott

Clichy

Djourou

Song

Sagna

Almunia (GK)

Well, Clive, it's another big challenge for Shelby Town. Arsenal have injury worries up front but Wenger has faith in his young players. The lad Vela has a wonderful left foot and Theo Walcott will be a danger as always. I just wonder if young Dolan might be able to worry that reshuffled Arsenal defence. A star of the future for Town, that boy.

Team Talk

 The Shelby Town players are lined up in a 4-4-2 formation. If you imagine a mirror line from the goalkeeper to the central spot you will see that the formation is symmetrical. What is symmetry?

 Can you draw 10 players in a different formation so that they are symmetrical? Where is the mirror line?

Warm Up

▶ **Double multiples of 10 to 1000 and find corresponding halves**

1 Double

    a) 460   **b)** 230   **c)** 580   **d)** 190   **e)** 720   **f)** 840   **g)** 960   **h)** 680

2 Halve

    a) 860   **b)** 760   **c)** 1120   **d)** 960   **e)** 1640   **f)** 1480   **g)** 1540   **h)** 1380

Skills Practice

▶ **Read and plot coordinates in the 1ˢᵗ quadrant**
▶ **Reflect simple shapes in a mirror line**

This newspaper diagram shows the 10 Shelby Town players (not including the goalkeeper) in a 4-1-3-2 formation.

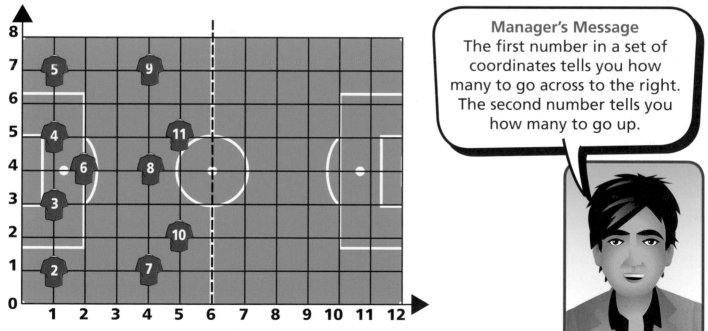

Manager's Message
The first number in a set of coordinates tells you how many to go across to the right. The second number tells you how many to go up.

1 Write the coordinates of each player.

2 Draw the same grid onto squared paper and use your coordinates to mark the players.

3 Now draw the opposition in the same formation, but an exact reflection of the Shelby Town team in the dotted mirror line marked.

4 Write the coordinates of the new team players.

Game On

▶ Draw coordinate grids

1 Copy Shelby Town in these formations and then draw the opposition in the same formation as an exact reflection in the mirror line. Make sure the players are drawn where the grid lines cross.

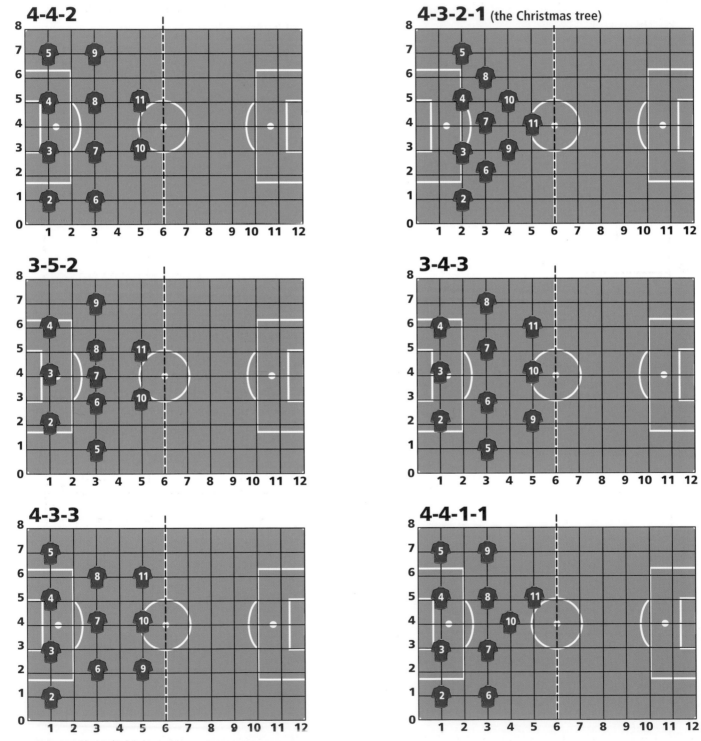

2 Write the coordinates of the players in both teams.
3 Talk to a partner about any patterns you notice.

The Big Match - Formation Coordination

Work with a partner. You will need 20 small counters.
You will need the Shelby Town cards marked from 1 to 11.

- Choose which half of the pitch each player will have.

- Each player should place ten counters in a formation of their choice in their half of the pitch. Do not have any players at the edge of the pitch.

- The two formations do not have to be reflections of each other.

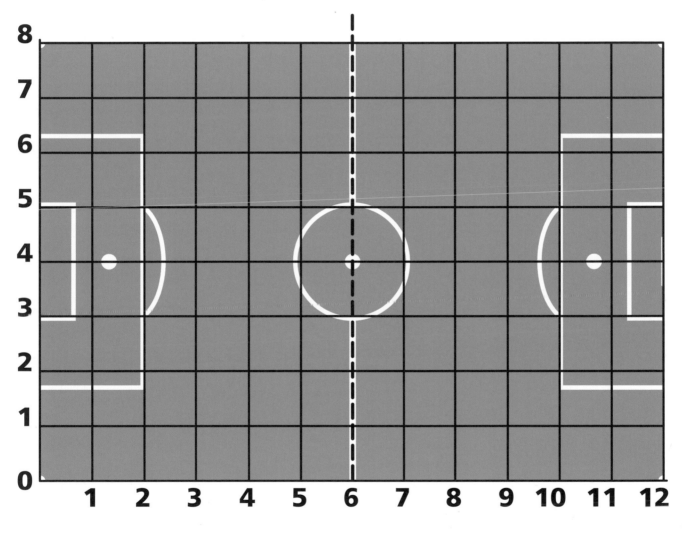

Kick-off

- Take turns to choose a number between 1 and 7. This will be the y-coordinate.

- Now pick a Shelby card to make the x-coordinate.

- Write down the pair of coordinates, making sure that you write the x-coordinate first.

- If a counter is on that position, remove it.

- Keep going until one team has left the pitch by all their counters being removed.

New Message

Send Chat Attach Address Fonts Colors Save As Draft

To:	Mick Diamond
Cc:	All training ground staff
Bcc:	
Subject:	Press Day
From:	Sandy Lane, Press Office

Hi Mick,

Just to confirm we have set up the press day for the new facilities at the training ground. Next Friday, after training. Hope we'll have enough space for all the reporters and photographers now! I have told people to get there for 1 p.m. so they won't be in your way before lunchtime. I'll have refreshments on tables around the main meeting room for them. When you and the players are ready, come over to the new conference area for the interviews.

I've spoken to Stuart Dolan, Dave Morgan and Jim Macdonald. They will be available for photos between 2 p.m. and 2.30 p.m. We want snaps of the new gym area in particular. This is good publicity and shows how far we have come as a club. I want us to grab plenty of space on those back pages!

The Chairman will join you at the training ground for lunch and the interviews afterwards. Hope that's OK. Let me know if there any problems. See you at the Fans Forum at the ground tonight.

Sandy

Team Talk

⚽ What does the word 'area' mean? Can you think of different areas in your school or house?

⚽ How do we measure area?

⚽ What is the difference between area and perimeter?

Warm Up

▶ **Round large positive numbers to the nearest 10, 100, 1000**

The attendances at several Premier League grounds are listed below.
Round them to the nearest 10, then 100, then 1000.

1 38 508	2 43 956	3 37 285	4 18 537	5 66 397

Skills Practice 1

▶ **Use the formula for the area of a rectangle**

Find the area of each pitch.

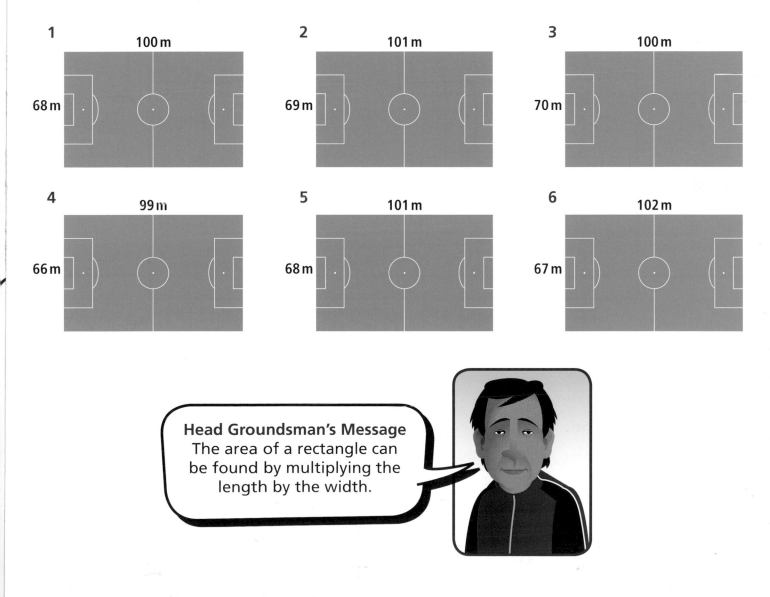

1 100 m, 68 m

2 101 m, 69 m

3 100 m, 70 m

4 99 m, 66 m

5 101 m, 68 m

6 102 m, 67 m

Head Groundsman's Message
The area of a rectangle can be found by multiplying the length by the width.

SPORT

May 13 • Daily News

10/10 DOLAN BOOSTS SHELBY TOWN SURVIVAL BID

'A huge result for us,' declared Shelby Town boss Mick Diamond, after watching his team snatch a vital win at Fulham. 'We've struggled lately but today we got back to doing what we do best. We got 8 out of 10 performances all over the pitch.'

It was one player's 10 out of 10 show that won Town the points, though. On the hour, Stuart Dolan created a goal out of nothing for his strike partner Tom Allenby. He picked up the ball on the halfway line and made a terrific diagonal run which had the Fulham defence on the back foot.

Dolan's passing was 80% accurate all afternoon and, this time, he slipped the perfect ball inside to midfielder Pierre Jean Vert. The Frenchman's shot hit Tom Allenby on the shoulder and spun up over Mark Schwarzer and in for the winner.

Mick Diamond was quick to praise the impact his teenage star has made: 'Stuart's still got a lot to learn but, in our position, we need one or two who can come in and play without fear.' Stuart Dolan's bravery – and his talent – may yet save Town from the drop!

Team Talk

 When there is lots of numerical data about teams and players we use 'averages' to summarise the data so that it is easier to understand. One average we use is called the 'mode'. Do you know what this is?

Sometimes it is easier to show information in a table or graph. What different types of graphs do you know?

Warm Up

▶ Add/subtract any pair of 2-digit numbers

1 46 + 27	2 38 + 14	3 29 + 43	4 68 + 25	5 48 + 33	6 37 + 56
7 46 - 27	8 38 - 14	9 69 - 43	10 68 - 25	11 41 - 33	12 92 - 56

Skills Practice 1

▶ Understand and use the mode and range to describe sets of data

Stuart Dolan had an excellent match today and was given a performance rating of 10 out of 10. This list shows the performance rating Stuart was given (out of 10) in the last 30 matches he played in full.

8	3	4	5	6	6	5	3	6	5	5	6	7	7	4
6	4	7	6	7	8	6	9	8	8	9	7	7	8	10

1 What was

   a)   his highest rating?   b)   his lowest rating?   c)   the range of his ratings?

2 Copy and complete this table.

Rating	Tally	Frequency
3		
4		
5		
6		
7		
8		
9		
10		

> **Manager's Message**
> To find the range, subtract the lowest from the highest rating.

3 What is the mode? (The rating he got most often.)

4 Danny Smith's modal rating is 6 and his range is 4. Talk to a partner about these figures and compare them with Stuart Dolan's.

Skills Practice 2

▶ **Construct and interpret frequency tables and bar charts with grouped data**

Stuart Dolan had an excellent match today. He made 72 passes with a completion rate of 81%. This list shows the number of passes made by Stuart Dolan in the last 30 matches he played in full.

63	25	45	42	65	53	38	18	42	39	47	57	62	58	33
41	30	46	38	50	54	27	51	39	42	49	38	51	60	72

1 Copy and complete this frequency table, using equal class intervals to group the data.

Number of passes	Tally	Frequency
1–10		
11–20		
21–30		

2 Check that the total of all the frequencies is 30.

3 On squared paper, draw a bar chart of the information in the table.

Game On

The following list gives his percentage completed pass rate (showing what proportion of his passes went to a team mate).

56%	45%	62%	64%	55%	72%	67%	55%	42%	25%
65%	56%	67%	68%	81%	75%	62%	38%	67%	72%
79%	67%	81%	64%	73%	83%	59%	62%	73%	89%

1 What is   **a)** the modal rating?   **b)** the range?

2 Draw a frequency table, using equal class intervals to group the data.

Percentage	Tally	Frequency
21%–30%		

3 On squared paper, draw a bar chart of the information in the table.

The Big Match - Shelby Town Players

These are the ratings for the Shelby Town team for today's match.

Jenks	7
Jones	8
Ball	7
Sefton	6
Morgan	7
Hannesen	8

Smith	6
Dolan	10
Odegbame	9
Allenby	8
Dunne	7
Dove (sub)	9

These are the ratings for last week's match.

Jenks	8
Jones	5
Ball	7
Sefton	8
Morgan	4
Hannesen	8

Smith	3
Dolan	8
Odegbame	9
Allenby	5
Dunne	6
Dove (sub)	6

Kick-off

- With a partner, compare the ratings for the two matches and write a report for the local newspaper.
- Include information about the mode and range for each match.
- Make judgements about what the data tells you.
- Find the total number of the ratings for each match. What does this show?
- Draw two bar charts of the information to include in your report.

Extra Time

Find some ratings for the players of several teams in the sports pages of a newspaper and write a similar report about the teams' performances.

Rob Mills (Presenter): Thanks Emma. More travel coming up in half an hour on BBC Radio Leeside. Back to our phone-in feature now. Remember you can call anytime on 01929 700600 and be part of the show. We're talking about Shelby Town's fantastic season. Delighted to say we're joined now by the gaffer himself, Mick Diamond.

Mick: Hello Rob.

Rob: You must be the happiest man in Shelby. What's the secret of Town's success this season? Not many gave you a chance of staying up, did they?

Mick: Well, we tried to win a big proportion of all our matches. It's no good hanging on for draws. The teams below us all lost fewer games than us but we won more than they did.

Rob: Three points for a win, of course.

Mick: Exactly. I'll take one win ahead of two draws every day! So our thinking was to go out and try to get goals. Odegbame, Allenby and Dolan did the business for us. Never mind the games we lost or drew. It was the high proportion of wins we got from our games which kept us up.

Rob: And kept the Manor Park crowd entertained, too.

Mick: Absolutely. And we'll go for it again next season as well!

Rob: Great stuff, Mick. It's been good talking to you. That's Mick Diamond, Manager of Shelby Town. Time now for you to have your say on BBC Radio Leeside. Call 01929 700600. This is Chris from Dagton. Hello Chris. What have you got to say?

Team Talk

 Proportion is how a whole is split up. We can describe the proportion of all the matches Shelby have played that they have won, lost or drawn.

 Proportions are sometimes described as fractions and sometimes as percentages.

Warm Up

▶ **Derive division facts associated with the multiplication tables**

| 1 | 24 ÷ 2 | 2 | 12 ÷ 4 | 3 | 24 ÷ 3 | 4 | 24 ÷ 6 | 5 | 36 ÷ 6 |

| 6 | 36 ÷ 4 | 7 | 24 ÷ 8 | 8 | 12 ÷ 3 | 9 | 36 ÷ 9 | 10 | 360 ÷ 4 |

Skills Practice

▶ **Interpret simple pie charts**

The results of the first 12 matches of Shelby Town's season are shown in this pie chart.

1 What fraction of the matches were

   a) draws?   **b)** wins?   **c)** losses?

2 How many of the matches were

   a) draws?   **b)** wins?   **c)** losses?

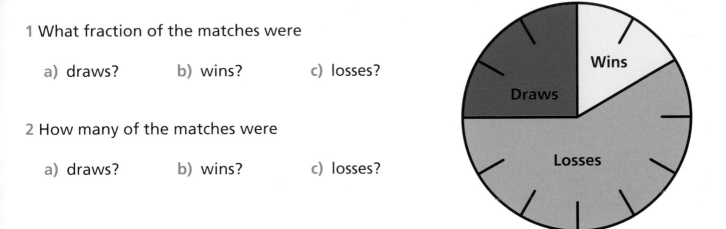

The results of the first 24 matches of Shelby Town's season are shown in this pie chart.

3 What fraction of the matches were

   a) draws?   **b)** wins?   **c)** losses?

4 How many of the matches were

   a) draws?   **b)** wins?   **c)** losses?

5 After their 12th match, how many more matches did they draw, win and lose up to and including their 24th match?

Game On

▶ Interpret pie charts
▶ Solve problems involving proportions

These pie charts show the results of several teams near the end of a season, having each played 36 matches.

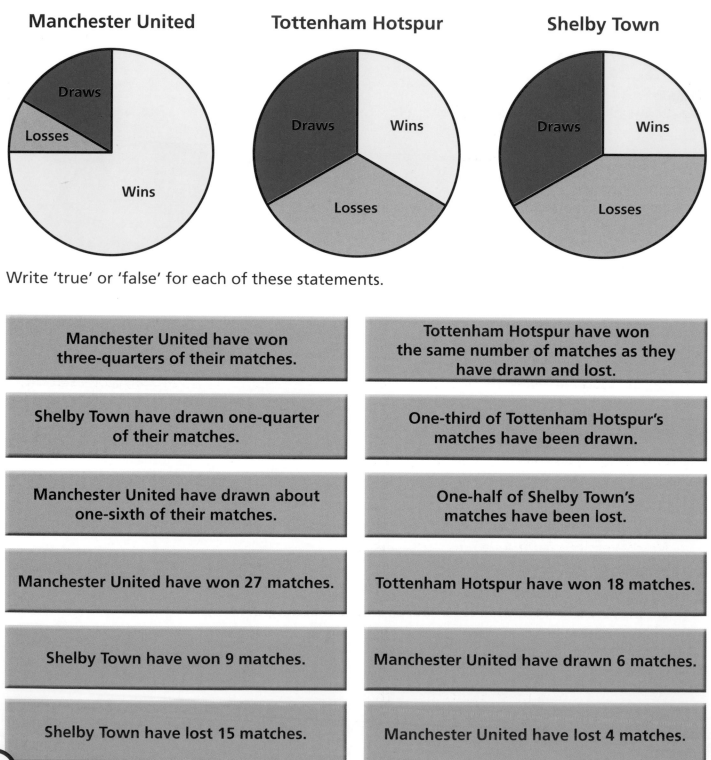

Manchester United   Tottenham Hotspur   Shelby Town

Write 'true' or 'false' for each of these statements.

Manchester United have won three-quarters of their matches.	Tottenham Hotspur have won the same number of matches as they have drawn and lost.
Shelby Town have drawn one-quarter of their matches.	One-third of Tottenham Hotspur's matches have been drawn.
Manchester United have drawn about one-sixth of their matches.	One-half of Shelby Town's matches have been lost.
Manchester United have won 27 matches.	Tottenham Hotspur have won 18 matches.
Shelby Town have won 9 matches.	Manchester United have drawn 6 matches.
Shelby Town have lost 15 matches.	Manchester United have lost 4 matches.

The Big Match –
Place Value Penalty Shoot-out

These pie charts show the proportion of players from different parts of the world for four clubs.
Each pie chart represents the 24 players in each squad.

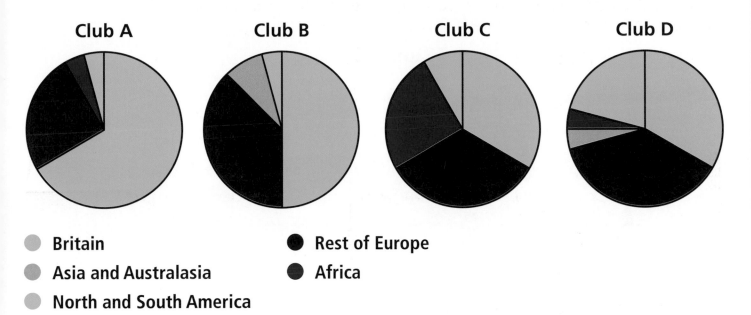

Club A   **Club B**   **Club C**   **Club D**

● Britain   ● Rest of Europe
● Asia and Australasia   ● Africa
● North and South America

Kick-off

- Each player should choose a club from above.
- Go through each statement below. If the statement is true for your club, score a point.
- The winner is the player with the most points at the end.

> *Over half of the squad are from Britain.*
> *One-quarter of the squad are from Africa.*
> *Eight players in the squad are from Britain.*
> *About three-quarters of the squad are from Europe (including Britain).*
> *More players are from Asia and Australasia than from Africa.*
> *No players are from Asia and Australasia.*
> *No players are from Africa.*
> *More players are from North and South America than from Asia and Australasia.*
> *Six players are from the rest of Europe (not including Britain).*
> *There are the same number of players from Britain as from the rest of Europe.*

- Choose two other clubs and play again.
- Which club scores most points altogether?

Show me

Resources: pack of Shelby Town cards

- Play this game in a pair.
- Player 1 chooses a description from the list below.

Show me a 2-digit odd number.

Show me a multiple of 8.

Show me a number greater than 10 and less than 15 that is a multiple of 4.

Show me a single-digit odd number that, when rounded to the nearest 10, rounds to 10.

- Player 2 finds a card in the pack that fits the description. Are there any more cards that fit?
- Take turns until you have worked your way through all the descriptions.

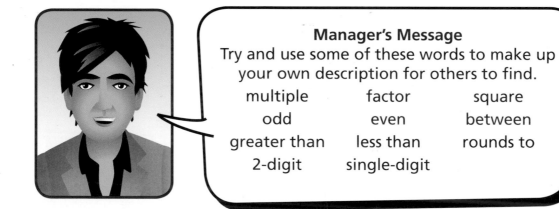

Manager's Message
Try and use some of these words to make up your own description for others to find.

multiple	factor	square
odd	even	between
greater than	less than	rounds to
2-digit	single-digit	

Final score

Resources: pack of Shelby Town cards

Manager's Message
Play the game again using different rules for scoring points.

- Play this game in two teams.
- One player from each team picks a card, e.g. 12 and 15.
- Use the rules below to calculate what your card scores.

Multiple of 5 scores 5 points.

Even number scores 1 point.

Multiple of 3 scores 3 points.

For example, 12 is an even number (1 point) and a multiple of 3 (3 points), so the card scores 4 points.

- Keep on playing until everyone in both teams has picked a card. Keep score to see which team ends up with the highest total.